Southern Living®

INCREDIBLE

COOKIES

Brownie Cookies
(page 44)

Southern Living®

INCREDIBLE

COOKIES

Oxmoor House®

Southern Living® Incredible Cookies

Book Division of Southern Progress Corporation
P.O. Box 2463, Birmingham, AL 35201

Created especially for *Southern Living At Home*™,
the Direct Selling Division of Southern Progress Corporation

For information about *Southern Living At Home*™, please write to:
Consultant Services
P.O. Box 830951
Birmingham, AL 35282-8451

Library of Congress Control Number: 00-091846
ISBN: 0-8487-2389-9
Printed in the United States of America
Third Printing 2002

Cover: *Starfish Sugar Cookies (page 18)*
Back Cover: *Brownie Cookies (page 44)*

Oxmoor House, Inc.
Editor-in-Chief: Nancy Fitzpatrick Wyatt
Senior Foods Editor: Susan Carlisle Payne
Senior Editor, Copy and Homes: Olivia Kindig Wells
Art Director: James Boone

Southern Living At Home™
Vice President and Executive Director: Dianne Mooney
Design Editor: Linda Baltzell Wright

Southern Living® Incredible Cookies
Editor: Julie Gunter
Associate Art Director: Cynthia R. Cooper
Designer: Clare T. Minges
Senior Copy Editor: Keri Bradford Anderson
Editorial Assistants: Jane E. Lorberau, Suzanne Powell
Test Kitchens Director: Elizabeth T. Luckett
Assistant Test Kitchens Director: Julie Christopher
Recipe Editor: Gayle Hays Sadler
Test Kitchens Staff: Rebecca Mohr Boggan;
Gretchen Feldtman, R.D.; David Gallent;
Kathleen Royal Phillips; Jan A. Smith
Senior Photographer: Jim Bathie
Photographers: Ralph Anderson, Tina Cornett, Brit Huckabay
Senior Photo Stylist: Kay E. Clarke
Photo Stylists: Virginia R. Cravens, Leslie Byars Simpson
Director, Production and Distribution: Phillip Lee
Associate Production Manager: Greg Amason
Production Assistant: Faye Porter Bonner

CONTENTS

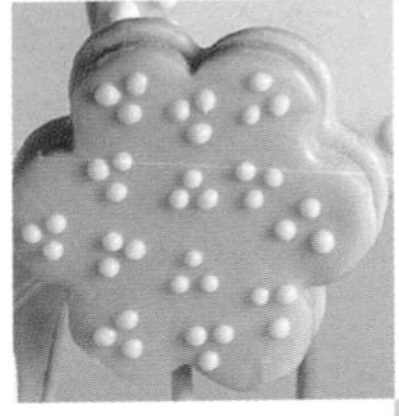

COOKIE
primer

Follow our tips for measuring, rolling, cutting, baking, and decorating flawless cookies every time. And check out some innovative ideas for cookie cutters.

◀ Use stainless steel or plastic measuring cups to measure dry ingredients. For flour, lightly spoon it into cup, letting it mound slightly; then level the top (shown at right).

When measuring dry ▶ ingredients, level the top using the straight edge of a spatula or knife.

To measure brown sugar ▶ accurately, use the measuring cup that holds the exact amount called for in a recipe. Pack brown sugar firmly into dry measuring cup; then level it off.

Butter, margarine, and shortening are all available as sticks marked in tablespoon increments for easy measuring. Use a knife and be exact in cutting just the right amount needed for a recipe.

Measure liquids in a glass or clear plastic measuring cup with a pouring lip. Read liquid measurements at eye level.

Roll cookie dough to an even and precise thickness using rubber rolling pin rings. Or use a ruler to check thickness of dough after rolling.

Punch cookie cutter quickly into dough, and promptly remove cutter. Make cutouts close together to get maximum yield from dough.

Dip cookie cutter in flour between cutouts to prevent sticking.

A tip from cookie baking pros: Once you've rolled and cut cookies and placed them on baking sheets, place baking sheets in the refrigerator or freezer 5 to 10 minutes to help set the shape before baking.

Use a wide spatula or dough scraper to transfer dough cutouts to baking sheet. Place cutouts several inches apart on baking sheet to allow for spreading during baking.

If you don't have cookie cutters handy, use a fluted pastry wheel to cut out cookie "sticks."

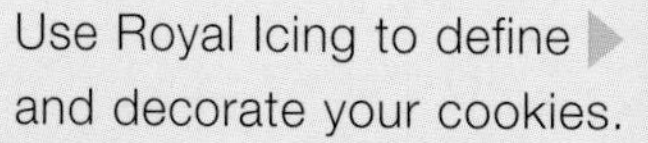

Use Royal Icing to define and decorate your cookies.

Cookies are easy to transfer to wire racks when you bake them on parchment paper-lined baking sheets. And cleanup's easy, too!

When making drop cookies, spoon dough evenly onto baking sheet as specific recipes direct. A cookie scoop easily measures tablespoon portions. Otherwise, use two spoons—one to scoop the dough, the other to push the dough off the spoon onto the baking sheet.

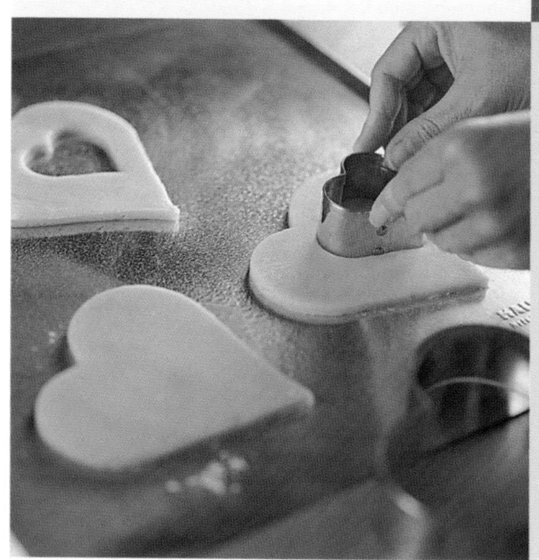

To make sandwich cookies with a window, use two sizes of the same cutter. Bake some solid cookies and some cutout cookies. Spread chocolate or your favorite jam on the solid cookies; top with cutout cookies.

Use decorative cutters to cut out shapes from a pan of fudgy brownies. Just line the pan with foil before baking; then lift uncut baked brownies from pan and cut out shapes.

COOKIE STORAGE HINTS

- Cool cookies completely before storing.
- Separate moist or sticky cookies with layers of wax paper.
- Store soft cookies in an airtight container. If cookies harden, soften them again by placing an apple wedge on a piece of wax paper in the container. (Be sure to remove the apple after one day.)
- Store crisp cookies in a container with a loose-fitting lid.
- Double-bag cookies in zip-top plastic bags for freezing. For crisp cookies, bring to room temperature; then reheat at 325° for 3 to 5 minutes.

Make ice cream sandwiches using cookie cutters. Bake a batch of cookies using a 3-inch round cutter to shape them; then spread 3 to 4 cups of ice cream in a plastic wrap-lined 9-inch cakepan, and freeze. Unmold ice cream, and use the same cutter to cut out circles. Assemble sandwiches.

Use various shapes and sizes of cookie cutters to cut out bread for shapely French toast or party tea sandwiches.

COLORING SUGAR

You can color your own sugar by stirring together 1 cup sugar and 5 drops liquid food coloring. Let dry, and store in an airtight container. Use colored sugar to decorate holiday cookies.

Sugar Cookie Centerpiece (page 14)

chapter

1

rolled & cut cookies

The versatile dough below makes a variety of impressive sugar cookies. The dippable Glaze and easy Royal Icing will transform the cookies into works of art almost too pretty to eat. Use the glaze to dip and coat cookies in a solid color; use the icing to make a detailed outline over the glaze or to decorate elaborate cookies in several colors. Refer to these recipes for decorating ideas throughout this chapter.

CLASSIC SUGAR COOKIES

1 cup butter or margarine, softened
1 cup sugar
1 large egg
1 teaspoon vanilla extract
3 cups all-purpose flour
¼ teaspoon salt

Beat butter at medium speed with an electric mixer 2 minutes or until creamy. Gradually add sugar, beating well. Add egg and vanilla, beating well. Gradually add flour and salt, beating until blended. Divide dough in half; cover and chill 1 hour.

Roll each portion of dough to ¼-inch thickness on a lightly floured surface. Cut with desired cookie cutters. Place on lightly greased baking sheets.

Bake at 350° for 8 to 10 minutes or until edges of cookies are lightly browned. Cool cookies 1 minute on baking sheets; remove to wire racks to cool completely.

See specific instructions on pages 13 through 21 for decorating ideas and for individual cookie recipe yields.

GLAZE

1 (16-ounce) package powdered sugar
6 tablespoons warm water
Liquid food coloring (optional)

Stir together powdered sugar and warm water using a wire whisk. Divide and tint with food coloring, if desired; place in shallow bowls for ease in dipping cookies. Yield: 1⅓ cups.

ROYAL ICING

1 (16-ounce) package powdered sugar
3 tablespoons meringue powder
5 to 6 tablespoons warm water
1 teaspoon light corn syrup
Paste food coloring (optional)

Combine first 4 ingredients in a large bowl. Beat at medium-low speed with an electric mixer 5 to 7 minutes. Divide and tint with food coloring, if desired. Icing dries quickly, so keep it covered at all times. Yield: 1⅔ cups.

OUTLINING DIRECTIONS:

Spoon Royal Icing into a pastry bag fitted with a small round tip, such as No. 2, 3, or 4—the smaller the number, the finer the outline. (If you don't have decorating tips, pour icing into a heavy-duty zip-top plastic bag; seal bag, and snip a tiny hole in 1 corner.) Touch the point of the tip where you want outline to start, and squeeze bag to let a little icing flow. Continue squeezing bag, and draw tip across cookie where you want icing. To end the line, touch the tip where you want it to end, and release pressure on bag. To draw a straight line, pull the icing through the air just above the cookie, rather than touching the cookie.

FLOW-IN ICING DIRECTIONS:

Spoon about a third of each desired color Royal Icing into pastry bag fitted with a coupler and a small round tip, such as No. 2, 3, or 4. (The coupler helps you interchange tips to bags of different color icing.) Slowly stir enough water into the remaining two-thirds of each desired color icing until it "flows" into a smooth surface after stirring. Spoon the thinned flow-in icing into a pastry bag without a tip; snip a small hole in 1 corner of bag just before piping.

Using undiluted Royal Icing, outline cookie or desired shape(s) within cookie. Using flow-in icing, pipe icing to cover areas within outlines as desired; spread icing into corners and hard-to-reach areas using a wooden pick. If air bubbles form, puncture them with wooden pick. Add flow-in icing, 1 color at a time, allowing icing to dry before changing colors.

SUGAR COOKIE CENTERPIECE

(shown on page 10): Cut dough for Classic Sugar Cookies (page 12) into desired shapes, using floured 2½-inch cookie cutters or paper patterns. Place on lightly greased baking sheets. Bake at 350° for 8 to 10 minutes. Cool completely before decorating.

Dip cookies in white or pastel Glaze (page 12); let dry. To tint 1 recipe of Glaze for each color, use the following: 2 drops red for pink; 2 drops blue for blue; 2 drops blue plus 2 drops red for purple; 2 drops red plus 3 drops yellow for orange.

Outline cookies as desired with Royal Icing (recipe and Outlining Directions, previous page). Let dry.

To make lollipop cookies, spread 1 tablespoon icing on back of 1 cookie. Place end of a ⅛-inch dowel over icing; roll dowel in icing to saturate. Place second cookie over dowel, right side up; press gently. Let dry 2 days.

To make lollipop cookies into a centerpiece, wedge a block of florist foam in a flower pot. Insert each cookie stem securely into foam. Use shredded paper or curly ribbon to cover florist foam. Yield: 42 (2½-inch) cookies or 21 lollipop sandwich cookies.

ALPHABET SUGAR COOKIES

(shown at right): Cut dough for Classic Sugar Cookies (page 12) using 3-inch alphabet cutters. Place on lightly greased baking sheets. Bake at 350° for 8 to 10 minutes. Cool completely before decorating.

For simple decorations, dip cookies in white or tinted Glaze (page 12); let dry completely. Add detail using desired color Royal Icing (previous page) and small round tips, such as No. 2, 3, or 4. For the ruffly outline on the Y and N, use tip No. 13. For the design on the T, dip the cookie in tinted glaze, sprinkle with colored sugar, and outline using Royal Icing and tip No. 3. For the design on the L, spread cookie with melted vanilla candy coating, add drops of melted chocolate candy coating, and drag a wooden pick through both to create a marbled pattern.

For more detailed decorations, such as the H, decorate exclusively with Royal Icing. Outline the cookie using tip No. 3; add detail within the cookie using tip No. 3 for the single lines and basket weave tip No. 47 for the thicker rippled stripes. Then fill in spaces with flow-in icing (Flow-in Icing Directions, previous page.) Yield: 32 cookies.

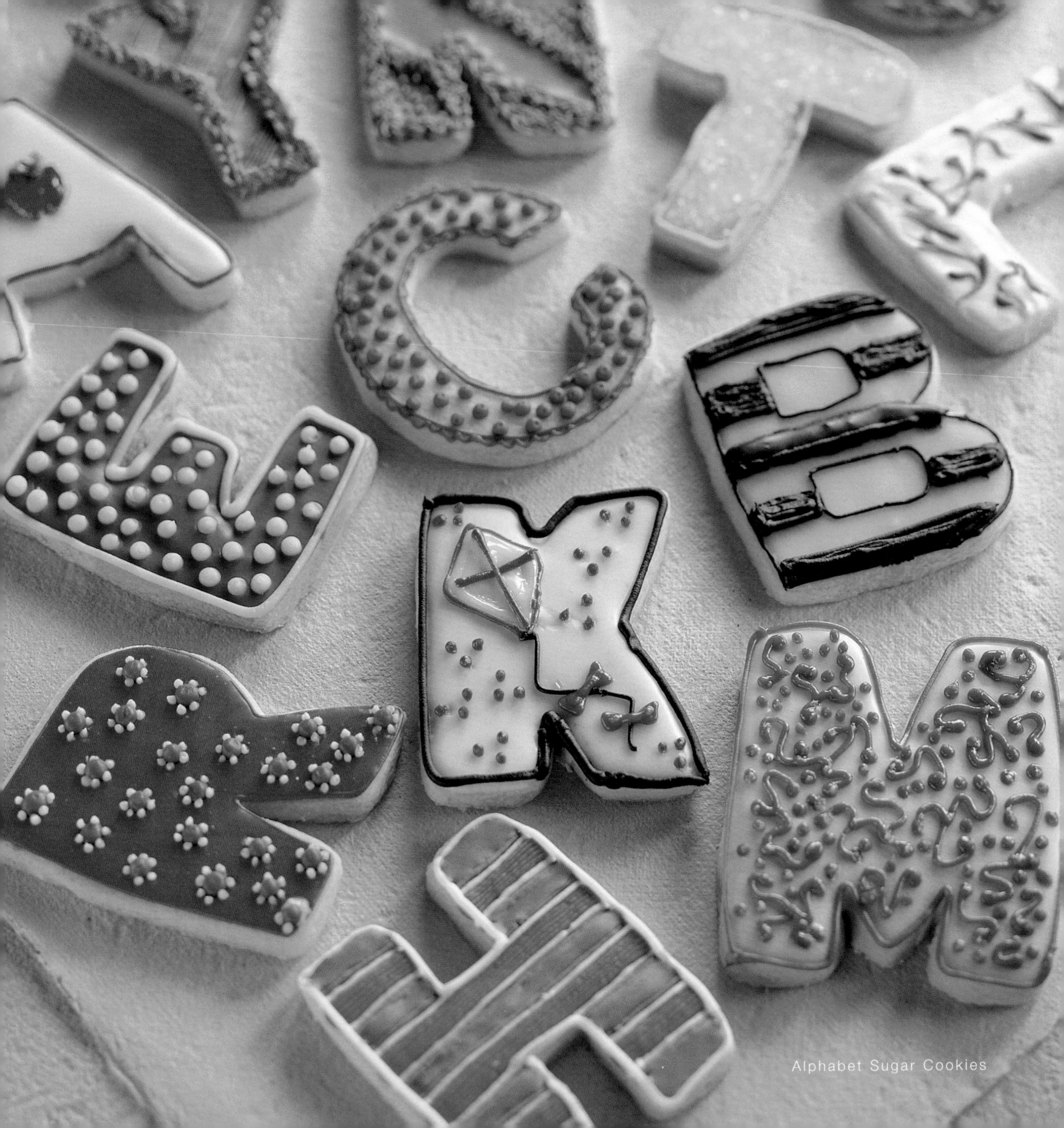

Alphabet Sugar Cookies

Celebration Cake Cookies

CELEBRATION CAKE COOKIES

Cut dough for Classic Sugar Cookies (page 12) using 3½-inch wedding cake cutter. Place on lightly greased baking sheets. Bake at 350° for 11 to 12 minutes or until edges are barely browned. Cool completely before decorating.

Dip cookies in white or pastel Glaze (page 12) to make a bride's cake or in brown Glaze for a groom's cake; let dry completely.

Outline cookies, and decorate as desired with white Royal Icing (recipe and Outlining Directions, page 13) using small round tips, such as No.1, 2, 3, or 4. Tint Royal Icing brown to decorate groom's cake. Tint icing with pastel colors and use tip No. 81 or a fluted tip such as No. 13 to make flowers and other designs on cookies.

You can also decorate cookies made with this cutter for a birthday, anniversary, or bridal luncheon. Write names on individual cookies, and present them as place cards or party favors. Yield: 19 cookies.

STARFISH SUGAR COOKIES

Cut dough for Classic Sugar Cookies (page 12) using 5-inch starfish cutter. Place on lightly greased baking sheets. Bake at 350° for 8 to 10 minutes. Cool completely before decorating.

Dip cookies in Glaze (page 12) and sprinkle, while Glaze is still wet, with sparkling white sugar, edible glitter, or turbinado sugar.

For more detailed decorations, outline plain cookies with Royal Icing (recipe and Outlining Decorations, page 13) using tip No. 3; then pipe decorative dots as desired. Or outline cookies with Royal Icing, and fill in spaces with flow-in icing (Flow-in Icing Directions, page 13) to create more dimensional starfish. Sprinkle with desired sugars. Yield: 20 cookies.

Starfish Sugar Cookies

Ice Cream
Cone Cookies

ICE CREAM CONE COOKIES

Cut dough for Classic Sugar Cookies (page 12) using 4-inch ice cream cone cutter. Place on lightly greased baking sheets. Bake at 350° for 8 to 10 minutes. Cool completely before decorating.

To decorate cones, brush cone portion with white Glaze (page 12); sprinkle with turbinado sugar. For another cone design, brush cone portion with brown Glaze, and sprinkle with chocolate sprinkles. For other cone designs, pipe cone portion to make a webbed design with dark brown Royal Icing using a small round tip, such as No. 2, 3, or 4.

To decorate "simple" ice cream tops: spread tops with white Glaze, and sprinkle with crushed hard peppermint candy or crushed chocolate sandwich cookies. For fudge swirl ice cream: spread top of cookie with white Glaze, add dots of melted chocolate candy coating to wet Glaze, and drag a wooden pick through both to create swirls.

To decorate "fancy" ice cream tops: outline tops with desired color Royal Icing (page 13); fill in spaces with same color flow-in icing (Flow-in Icing Directions, page 13). Sprinkle wet icing with colored sprinkles, if desired. Yield: 44 cookies.

CHOCOLATE FLEUR-DE-LIS COOKIES

- 1½ cups butter or margarine, softened
- 2½ cups sifted powdered sugar
- 2 large eggs
- 1 teaspoon vanilla extract
- 3 cups all-purpose flour
- 1 cup Dutch cocoa
- ¼ teaspoon salt
- ½ teaspoon ground cinnamon
- Royal Icing (page 13)
- Edible gold luster dust

Beat butter at medium speed with an electric mixer until creamy; gradually add powdered sugar, beating well. Add eggs and vanilla; beat until blended.

Combine flour and next 3 ingredients. Gradually add to butter mixture, beating at low speed until blended. (Dough will be soft.) Divide dough in half; wrap each portion tightly in plastic wrap. Chill at least 1 hour.

Roll 1 portion at a time to ¼-inch thickness on a floured surface. Cut dough with a floured 4-inch fleur-de-lis-shaped cutter; place on ungreased baking sheets. If you want to attach a ribbon to finished cookies, poke holes in tops of dough cutouts using a plastic drinking straw or the end of a wooden spoon.

Bake at 350° for 10 minutes. Cool 3 minutes on baking sheets; remove to wire racks to cool completely.

Decorate cookies with Royal Icing, or lightly brush them with gold luster dust. (See bottom left photo on opposite page.) Yield: 22 cookies.

Vanilla Fleur-de-lis Cookies: Prepare Classic Sugar Cookie dough (page 12). Cut dough using fleur-de-lis-shaped cutter. Place on lightly greased baking sheets. Bake at 350° for 10 to 12 minutes. Cool 1 minute on baking sheets; remove to wire racks to cool completely. Lightly brush cookies with gold luster dust, or decorate with Royal Icing. Yield: 1 dozen.

Fleur-de-lis Cookies

LEMON-POPPY SEED COOKIES

The absence of butter in this simple cookie gives it an appealing cracker-like texture.

2 cups all-purpose flour
1½ teaspoons baking powder
½ teaspoon salt
1½ teaspoons poppy seeds
1 large egg
¾ cup sugar
⅓ cup heavy whipping cream
1 tablespoon grated lemon rind
Sugar

Combine first 4 ingredients; set aside. Beat egg in a large mixing bowl at medium speed with an electric mixer. Gradually add sugar and whipping cream, beating well. Stir in flour mixture and lemon rind. Cover and chill dough at least 1 hour.

Divide dough in half. Work with 1 portion of dough at a time, storing remaining dough in refrigerator.

Roll each portion of dough to ⅛-inch thickness on a floured surface. Cut with 3-inch alphabet cookie cutters, and place cookies on lightly greased baking sheets. Sprinkle with sugar.

Bake at 350° for 8 to 9 minutes or until barely browned. Cool slightly on baking sheets; remove to wire racks to cool completely. Yield: about 2 dozen.

Lemon-Poppy Seed Cookies

OLD-FASHIONED TEA CAKES

- ½ cup butter, softened
- 1 cup sugar
- 2 large eggs
- 2½ cups all-purpose flour
- 2 teaspoons baking powder
- ½ teaspoon ground nutmeg
- 1 tablespoon milk

Beat butter at medium speed with an electric mixer until creamy; gradually add sugar, beating well. Add eggs, beating until blended.

Combine flour, baking powder, and nutmeg; add to butter mixture alternately with milk, beginning and ending with flour mixture. Beat at low speed just until blended after each addition.

Divide dough in half; cover with plastic wrap, and chill 1 hour. Roll each portion of dough to ¼-inch thickness on a floured surface. Cut with a 2¼-inch round cutter, and place on greased baking sheets. Bake at 350° for 8 minutes. (Cookies will be pale.) Cool 1 minute on baking sheets; remove to wire racks to cool completely. Yield: 3½ dozen.

BROWN SUGAR COOKIE HOUSES

- 1 cup butter, softened
- 1½ cups firmly packed dark brown sugar
- 1 large egg
- 1 teaspoon vanilla extract
- 3⅓ cups all-purpose flour
- 1 teaspoon baking soda
- ½ teaspoon salt
- Glaze (page 12)
- Royal Icing (page 13)
- Fresh herbs (optional)

Beat butter at medium speed with an electric mixer until creamy. Gradually add brown sugar, beating well. Add egg and vanilla, beating well.

Combine flour, soda, and salt; add to butter mixture, beating just until blended. Dough may appear crumbly. Use hands to knead and shape dough into a ball; divide in half. Roll each portion of dough to ¼-inch thickness between 2 sheets of wax paper. Cut with a 4-inch house-shaped cookie cutter. Place 1 inch apart on ungreased baking sheets.

Bake at 350° for 10 to 12 minutes. Cool 1 minute on baking sheets; carefully remove to wire racks to cool completely.

Dip cookies in Glaze, if desired. Divide Royal Icing and tint with paste food coloring. Use icing to outline houses, doors, windows, and rooftops. Make flow-in icing to create "stonework" on house where desired (Flow-in Icing Directions, page 13). Add tiny sprigs of herbs to window box, if desired. Yield: 19 cookies.

GINGERBREAD SNOWFLAKE COOKIES

1 cup butter or margarine, softened
1 cup sugar
¼ cup water
1½ teaspoons baking soda
1 cup molasses
5 cups all-purpose flour
¼ teaspoon salt
1½ tablespoons ground ginger
½ teaspoon ground allspice
1½ teaspoons ground cinnamon
Royal Icing (page 13)
Sparkling white sugar (optional)
Powdered sugar

Beat butter and sugar at medium speed with an electric mixer until fluffy (3 to 4 minutes). Stir together ¼ cup water and baking soda until dissolved; stir in molasses.

Combine flour and next 4 ingredients. Add to butter mixture alternately with molasses mixture, beginning and ending with flour mixture. Shape dough into a ball; cover and chill 1 hour.

Roll dough to ¼-inch thickness on a lightly floured surface. Cut with a 5½-inch snowflake cookie cutter. Place 2 inches apart on parchment paper-lined baking sheets. Poke holes in snowflakes using a plastic drinking straw, if desired.

Bake at 350° for 12 minutes. Cool 1 minute on baking sheets; remove to wire racks to cool completely.

Spoon Royal Icing into a small heavy-duty zip-top plastic bag. Snip a tiny hole in 1 corner of bag, and outline and decorate cookies; sprinkle icing with sparkling sugar, if desired. Or sprinkle plain cookies with powdered sugar. Yield: 21 cookies.

Little Gingerbread Snowflake Cookies: Use a 3-inch cookie cutter. Bake 10 to 12 minutes. Sprinkle with powdered sugar, or decorate with Royal Icing and sparkling sugar. Yield: about 6 dozen.

Gingerbread
Snowflake Cookies

Kahlúa Wafers

KAHLÚA WAFERS

You can really taste the coffee flavor in these thin praline-like cookies "for adults only."

- ¾ cup butter, softened
- ¾ cup sugar
- 2 cups all-purpose flour
- ¼ teaspoon baking powder
- ½ teaspoon salt
- 3 tablespoons Kahlúa
- 2 tablespoons instant coffee granules
- 1 teaspoon vanilla extract
- 4 (2-ounce) squares chocolate or vanilla candy coating, melted

Beat butter at medium speed with an electric mixer until creamy; gradually add sugar, beating well.

Combine flour, baking powder, and salt in a medium bowl; add to butter mixture, beating at low speed just until blended.

Stir together Kahlúa, coffee granules, and vanilla until coffee granules dissolve. Add Kahlúa mixture to butter mixture, beating until blended.

Turn dough out onto a lightly floured surface, and roll to ⅛-inch thickness.

Cut dough with a floured 3-inch heart-shaped or round cutter, and place 1 inch apart on lightly greased baking sheets.

Bake at 375° for 7 minutes or until cookies are lightly browned; remove to wire racks to cool completely. Dip half of each cookie into melted candy coating. Place on wax paper to dry. Yield: 16 cookies.

ROSEMARY SHORTBREAD COOKIES

We recommend serving these wonderfully tender-crisp cookies with a cup of your favorite hot tea or atop a cool scoop of sherbet.

- ½ cup butter, softened
- ⅓ cup sifted powdered sugar
- 1½ cups all-purpose flour
- 2 tablespoons chopped fresh rosemary

Beat butter at medium speed with an electric mixer until creamy; gradually add sugar, beating well. Gradually add flour to butter mixture, beating at low speed until blended. Gently stir in rosemary.

Roll dough to ¼-inch thickness on a lightly floured surface. Cut with a 2-inch cookie cutter; place cutouts on lightly greased baking sheets. Bake at 325° for 16 to 18 minutes or until edges are lightly browned. Remove cookies to wire racks to cool completely. Yield: about 1 dozen.

Rosemary
Shortbread Cookies

BROWN SUGAR SHORTBREAD

- 1 cup butter, softened
- ½ cup firmly packed dark brown sugar
- 2 cups all-purpose flour
- 2 to 3 tablespoons sparkling white sugar

Beat butter at medium speed with an electric mixer until creamy; gradually add brown sugar, beating until light and fluffy. Gradually add flour, beating at low speed until smooth. Cover and chill dough 30 minutes.

Roll dough to ¼-inch thickness on a lightly floured surface. Cut with a 2-inch triangle-shaped cutter; place 1 inch apart on lightly greased baking sheets. Sprinkle with sparkling sugar.

Bake at 375° for 10 to 12 minutes or until edges are golden. Cool 5 minutes on baking sheets; remove to wire racks to cool completely. Yield: about 1½ dozen.

RUM-CURRANT SHORTBREAD

- ½ cup currants
- ¼ cup light rum
- 1 cup butter, softened
- ½ cup sifted powdered sugar
- 1¾ cups all-purpose flour
- ¼ teaspoon baking powder
- ¼ teaspoon salt

Bring currants and rum to a boil in a small saucepan. Remove from heat; cover and let stand 30 minutes. Drain currants, discarding rum, if desired.

Beat butter at medium speed with an electric mixer until creamy; gradually add powdered sugar, beating well.

Combine flour, baking powder, and salt; gradually add to butter mixture, beating at low speed until blended after each addition. Stir in currants. Cover and chill dough 30 minutes.

Roll dough to ¼-inch thickness on a lightly floured surface. Cut with a 2-inch round cutter; place 2 inches apart on lightly greased baking sheets.

Bake at 375° for 12 to 14 minutes or until edges just begin to brown. Cool 5 minutes on baking sheets; remove to wire racks to cool completely. Yield: 2 dozen.

Glazed Orange-Spice Cookies

GLAZED ORANGE-SPICE COOKIES

½ cup shortening
½ cup butter or margarine, softened
1 cup sugar
½ cup finely chopped almonds
3 tablespoons grated orange rind
1¾ cups all-purpose flour
1 teaspoon baking powder
½ teaspoon ground nutmeg
¼ teaspoon salt
¼ teaspoon ground cloves
¼ teaspoon ground cinnamon
2 cups sifted powdered sugar
⅔ cup orange marmalade
2 tablespoons orange juice
Garnish: sliced almonds

Beat shortening and butter at medium speed with an electric mixer until creamy; gradually add 1 cup sugar, beating well. Add ½ cup almonds and orange rind, beating well.

Combine flour and next 5 ingredients in a bowl; gradually add to shortening mixture, beating well.

Place dough on a lightly floured surface; roll into a 13½- x 12-inch rectangle. Cut into 3- x 1½-inch rectangles using a fluted pastry wheel or a knife; place on ungreased baking sheets. Bake at 350° for 12 to 13 minutes or until lightly browned. Cool slightly on baking sheets; remove to wire racks to cool completely.

Combine powdered sugar, marmalade, and orange juice; stir well. Spread glaze on cookies. Garnish, if desired. Yield: 3 dozen.

STRAWBERRY SANDWICH COOKIES

- ¼ cup plus 2 tablespoons butter, softened
- ¾ cup firmly packed brown sugar
- 1 large egg
- ¾ teaspoon vanilla extract
- 2 cups all-purpose flour
- ⅛ teaspoon salt
- ½ cup strawberry jam
- Powdered sugar

Beat butter at medium speed with an electric mixer until creamy; gradually add brown sugar, beating until light and fluffy. Add egg and vanilla, beating until blended.

Combine flour and salt; add to butter mixture, beating well. Divide dough in half, and wrap in wax paper. Chill 1 hour.

Roll half of dough to ⅛-inch thickness on a lightly floured surface; keep remaining dough chilled until ready to use. Cut with a 3½-inch round cookie cutter. Transfer cookies to lightly greased baking sheets.

Roll remaining half of dough to ⅛-inch thickness on a lightly floured surface. Cut with a 3½-inch round cookie cutter. Transfer cookies to lightly greased baking sheets. Cut out center of each cookie with a 1- or 1½-inch star-shaped cookie cutter.

Bake at 350° for 5 to 6 minutes or until cookies are lightly browned. Cool slightly on baking sheets; remove to wire racks to cool completely.

Spread solid cookies evenly with strawberry jam. Dust cookies with cutout centers lightly with powdered sugar. Top solid cookies with sugar-dusted cookies, pressing lightly together to fill cutouts with jam. Yield: about 2 dozen.

Strawberry
Sandwich Cookies

SOUR CREAM-NUTMEG SUGAR COOKIES

These fragrant, buttery cutouts are soft and thick like old-fashioned tea cakes your grandmother used to bake.

1 cup butter
1½ cups sugar
2 large eggs
1 cup sour cream
1½ teaspoons vanilla extract
4½ cups all-purpose flour
1 teaspoon baking powder
1 teaspoon baking soda
1 teaspoon salt
½ teaspoon ground nutmeg
Sugar

Beat butter at medium speed with an electric mixer until creamy; gradually add 1½ cups sugar, beating well. Add eggs, beating well. Add sour cream and vanilla, beating well.

Combine flour and next 4 ingredients; gradually add to butter mixture, beating well. Cover and chill at least 1 hour.

Divide dough into fourths. Work with 1 portion of dough at a time, storing remaining dough in refrigerator. Roll each portion to ¼-inch thickness on a lightly floured surface. Cut with a 3-inch cookie cutter; place on ungreased baking sheets. Sprinkle cookies with additional sugar.

Bake at 375° for 12 minutes or until lightly browned. Cool slightly on baking sheets; remove to wire racks to cool completely. Yield: 4 dozen.

TAIL WAGGERS

These little brown canine cookies are for your dog only.

- 2¼ cups whole wheat flour
- 1½ cups all-purpose flour
- 1½ cups cornmeal
- ¾ cup uncooked regular oats
- ⅓ cup instant nonfat dry milk powder
- 1 tablespoon garlic powder
- ½ teaspoon salt
- 1¾ cups beef broth
- ½ cup vegetable oil
- 2 large eggs
- 1 tablespoon Worcestershire sauce

Combine first 7 ingredients; make a well in center of dry ingredients.

Whisk together broth, oil, and 1 egg; add to dry ingredients, stirring until a soft dough forms.

Roll dough to ½-inch thickness on a lightly floured surface. Cut with a 4-inch dog bone-shaped cookie cutter, and place on ungreased baking sheets.

Whisk together remaining egg and Worcestershire sauce; brush on cookies.

Position oven racks to divide oven into thirds. Bake at 300° for 2 hours, placing a baking sheet on each rack. Turn oven off, and let cookies stay in oven with door closed 2 more hours. Yield: 40 (4-inch) canine cookies.

Jumbo Oatmeal-Butterscotch Chippers (page 45), Brownie Cookies (page 44)

chapter 2

drop cookies

BROWNIE COOKIES

These scrumptious double-chocolate cookies (shown on pages 2 and 42) are similar in texture to a fudgy brownie.

- ½ cup butter
- 4 (1-ounce) squares unsweetened chocolate, chopped
- 3 cups (18 ounces) semisweet chocolate morsels, divided
- 1½ cups all-purpose flour
- ½ teaspoon baking powder
- ½ teaspoon salt
- 4 large eggs
- 1½ cups sugar
- 2 teaspoons vanilla extract
- 2 cups chopped pecans, toasted

Combine butter, unsweetened chocolate, and 1½ cups chocolate morsels in a large heavy saucepan. Cook over low heat, stirring constantly, until butter and chocolate melt; cool.

Combine flour, baking powder, and salt in a small bowl; set aside.

Beat eggs, sugar, and vanilla at medium speed with an electric mixer. Gradually add dry ingredients to egg mixture, beating well. Add chocolate mixture; beat well. Stir in remaining 1½ cups chocolate morsels and pecans.

Drop dough by 2 tablespoonfuls 1 inch apart onto parchment paper-lined baking sheets.

Bake at 350° for 10 minutes. Cool slightly on baking sheets; remove to wire racks to cool completely. Yield: about 2½ dozen.

OATMEAL-BUTTERSCOTCH CHIPPERS

Oats take the place of flour in these crispy-edged butterscotch cookies (shown on page 42).

- 1¼ cups butter-flavored shortening
- 1¼ cups extra-crunchy peanut butter
- 1½ cups firmly packed brown sugar
- 1 cup sugar
- 3 large eggs
- 4½ cups uncooked regular oats
- 2 teaspoons baking powder
- 1½ cups (9 ounces) butterscotch morsels
- 1 cup (6 ounces) semisweet chocolate morsels
- 1 cup chopped pecans or pecan pieces

Beat shortening and peanut butter at medium speed with an electric mixer until creamy; gradually add sugars, beating well. Add eggs, 1 at a time, beating well after each addition.

Combine oats and baking powder; add to shortening mixture, beating well. Stir in butterscotch morsels, chocolate morsels, and pecans.

Drop dough by rounded teaspoonfuls onto ungreased baking sheets.

Bake at 350° for 9 to 11 minutes or until lightly browned. Cool 2 minutes on baking sheets; remove to wire racks to cool completely. Yield: 6 dozen.

Jumbo Oatmeal-Butterscotch Chippers: Drop dough by 2 tablespoonfuls 2 inches apart onto ungreased baking sheets. Bake at 350° for 11 to 12 minutes. Yield: 4½ dozen.

HEAVENLY CHOCOLATE CHUNK COOKIES

Mega-morsels give big chocolate taste to every bite of these deluxe chocolate chip cookies.

- ¾ cup butter or margarine
- 2 tablespoons instant coffee granules
- 2 cups plus 2 tablespoons all-purpose flour
- ½ teaspoon baking soda
- ½ teaspoon salt
- 1 cup firmly packed brown sugar
- ½ cup sugar
- 1 large egg
- 1 egg yolk
- 1 (11.5-ounce) package semisweet chocolate mega-morsels or chocolate chunks
- 1 cup walnut halves, toasted

Combine butter and coffee granules in a small saucepan or skillet. Cook over medium-low heat until butter melts and coffee granules dissolve, stirring occasionally. Remove from heat, and cool to room temperature (don't let butter resolidify).

Combine flour, baking soda, and salt; set aside.

Combine butter mixture, sugars, egg, and egg yolk in a large bowl. Beat at medium speed with an electric mixer until blended. Gradually add flour mixture, beating at low speed just until blended. Stir in chocolate mega-morsels and walnuts.

Drop dough by heaping tablespoonfuls 2 inches apart onto ungreased baking sheets.

Bake at 325° for 12 to 14 minutes. Cool cookies slightly on baking sheets. Remove to wire racks to cool completely. Yield: 20 cookies.

Heavenly Chocolate Chunk Cookies

TOASTED ALMOND AND CRANBERRY COOKIES

- ½ cup butter or margarine, softened
- ½ cup shortening
- 1 cup firmly packed brown sugar
- ⅔ cup sugar
- 2 large eggs
- 2 cups all-purpose flour
- 1 teaspoon baking powder
- ½ teaspoon baking soda
- ⅛ teaspoon salt
- 8 ounces premium white chocolate, chopped
- 2 cups corn flakes cereal
- 1 cup sliced almonds, lightly toasted
- 2 (3-ounce) packages dried cranberries
- ¾ teaspoon almond extract

Beat butter and shortening at medium speed with an electric mixer until creamy; gradually add sugars, beating well. Add eggs, beating well.

Combine flour, baking powder, soda, and salt; gradually add to butter mixture, beating well. Stir in chocolate, cereal, almonds, cranberries, and almond extract.

Drop dough by tablespoonfuls 2 inches apart onto ungreased baking sheets.

Bake at 350° for 10 minutes. Remove to wire racks to cool completely. Yield: 6 dozen.

ORANGE SLICE COOKIES

- 1½ cups chopped candy orange slices
- ¼ cup all-purpose flour
- 1 cup butter or margarine, softened
- 1 cup firmly packed brown sugar
- ¾ cup sugar
- 2 large eggs
- 2 tablespoons milk
- 2 teaspoons vanilla extract
- 2 cups all-purpose flour
- 1 teaspoon baking soda
- ½ teaspoon salt
- ½ teaspoon ground cinnamon
- ½ teaspoon ground nutmeg
- 2½ cups uncooked quick-cooking oats
- 1 cup flaked coconut

Combine chopped orange slices and ¼ cup flour in a medium bowl, tossing to coat candy; set aside. Beat butter at medium speed with an electric mixer until creamy; gradually add sugars, beating well. Add eggs, milk, and vanilla; beat well.

Combine 2 cups flour and next 4 ingredients; gradually add to butter mixture, beating well. Stir in candy mixture, oats, and coconut.

Drop dough by rounded teaspoonfuls 2 inches apart onto greased baking sheets.

Bake at 375° for 10 minutes or until lightly browned. Cool slightly on baking sheets; remove to wire racks to cool completely. Yield: 9 dozen.

JUMBO CHOCOLATE CHIP COOKIES

½ cup butter or margarine, softened
½ cup shortening
1 cup firmly packed brown sugar
½ cup sugar
2 large eggs
2 teaspoons vanilla extract
2½ cups all-purpose flour
1 teaspoon baking soda
½ teaspoon salt
2 cups (12 ounces) semisweet chocolate morsels
1 cup chopped pecans

Beat butter and shortening at medium speed with an electric mixer until creamy; gradually add sugars, beating well. Add eggs and vanilla, beating well.

Combine flour, soda, and salt; gradually add to butter mixture, beating well. Stir in chocolate morsels and pecans.

Drop dough by scant one-fourth cupfuls onto ungreased baking sheets; flatten each cookie into a 3½-inch circle, making sure flattened cookies are 2 inches apart.

Bake at 350° for 12 minutes. Cool slightly on baking sheets; remove to wire racks to cool completely. Yield: 2 dozen.

FRUITCAKE COOKIES

- 2 cups chopped pecans
- ½ pound candied pineapple, chopped
- ½ pound red and green candied cherries, chopped
- ½ pound golden raisins
- ¼ cup all-purpose flour
- ½ cup butter or margarine, softened
- 1 cup firmly packed brown sugar
- 4 large eggs
- 2½ cups all-purpose flour
- 1 teaspoon baking soda
- ¾ teaspoon ground cardamom

Combine first 5 ingredients in a large bowl, tossing to coat fruit and nuts with flour.

Beat butter at medium speed with an electric mixer until creamy; gradually add brown sugar, beating well. Add eggs, beating well.

Combine 2½ cups flour, baking soda, and cardamom in a bowl; gradually add to butter mixture, beating well. Stir in fruit mixture.

Drop dough by heaping teaspoonfuls 2 inches apart onto lightly greased baking sheets.

Bake at 350° for 12 minutes or until lightly browned. Cool slightly on baking sheets; remove to wire racks to cool completely. Yield: 9½ dozen.

FORGET 'EM COOKIES

Once you get these simple cookies in a hot oven, turn the oven off and forget 'em for eight hours.

- 2 egg whites
- ½ teaspoon vanilla extract
- ¼ teaspoon cream of tartar
- ½ cup sugar
- 1 cup (6 ounces) semisweet chocolate morsels
- 1 cup chopped pecans

Preheat oven to 350°. Beat first 3 ingredients at high speed with an electric mixer until foamy; gradually add sugar, 1 tablespoon at a time, beating until stiff peaks form and sugar dissolves (2 to 4 minutes).

Fold in semisweet chocolate morsels and pecans.

Drop mixture by heaping teaspoonfuls onto aluminum foil-lined baking sheets. Place in preheated 350° oven, and immediately turn off oven. Do not open oven door for at least 8 hours. Carefully remove cookies from foil. Store in an airtight container up to 1 week. Yield: 4½ dozen.

COCONUT MACAROONS

2⅔ cups shredded coconut
⅔ cup sugar
¼ cup all-purpose flour
¼ teaspoon salt
4 egg whites
1 teaspoon almond extract
1 cup slivered almonds

Combine first 4 ingredients in a bowl; stir well. Add egg whites and almond extract; stir well. Stir in almonds. Drop dough by teaspoonfuls onto greased baking sheets.

Bake at 325° for 22 minutes or until macaroons are golden. Remove immediately to wire racks to cool completely. Yield: 2 dozen.

Mixed Nut Turtles

MIXED NUT TURTLES

A patty of melted chocolate nestles between salty nuts on this candylike cookie.

¾ cup butter, softened
½ cup sugar
1 egg yolk
1 teaspoon vanilla extract
1½ cups all-purpose flour
1 (9.75-ounce) can mixed nuts (with almonds, macadamia nuts, and cashews)
1½ cups (9 ounces) semisweet chocolate morsels
2 teaspoons shortening

Beat butter at medium speed with an electric mixer until creamy. Gradually add sugar, beating well. Add egg yolk and vanilla, beating well. Add flour to butter mixture, beating just until blended.

Drop dough by level tablespoonfuls 2 inches apart onto ungreased baking sheets. Flatten each ball of dough to a 2-inch circle, using fingers.

Cut large macadamia nuts in half. Press nuts firmly into outside top edges of cookies.

Bake at 350° for 10 to 12 minutes or until edges are lightly browned. Cool 1 minute on baking sheets. Carefully remove cookies to wire racks to cool completely.

Place chocolate and shortening in top of a double boiler over hot water; stir until melted.

Spoon 1 heaping teaspoon melted chocolate onto center of each cookie. Spread and smooth chocolate between nuts. Let set until chocolate hardens. Yield: 26 cookies.

VANILLA-CHERRY COOKIES

1 (6-ounce) jar red maraschino cherries, drained
1 (6-ounce) jar green maraschino cherries, drained
½ cup butter or margarine, softened
½ cup shortening
1 (3-ounce) package cream cheese, softened
1 cup sugar
1 cup firmly packed brown sugar
2 large eggs
1½ teaspoons vanilla extract
2 cups all-purpose flour
1 teaspoon baking powder
½ teaspoon salt
1 cup uncooked quick-cooking oats
1 cup crisp rice cereal
1 cup chopped pecans
1 cup flaked coconut
1 (12-ounce) package vanilla morsels

Chop cherries; drain on paper towels. Set aside.

Beat butter, shortening, and cream cheese at medium speed with an electric mixer until creamy. Add sugars, beating well. Add eggs and vanilla, beating well.

Combine flour, baking powder, and salt; gradually add to butter mixture, beating well. Stir in cherries, oats, and remaining ingredients.

Drop dough by rounded tablespoonfuls 2 inches apart onto lightly greased baking sheets.

Bake at 350° for 12 minutes. Cool 1 minute on baking sheets; remove to wire racks to cool completely. Yield: about 4 dozen.

PECAN CRISPIES

½ cup butter, softened
½ cup shortening
2 cups firmly packed brown sugar
2 large eggs
2½ cups all-purpose flour
½ teaspoon baking soda
¼ teaspoon salt
1 cup chopped pecans

Beat butter and shortening at medium speed with an electric mixer until creamy; gradually add sugar, beating until fluffy. Add eggs; beat until blended.

Combine flour, soda, and salt; gradually add to butter mixture, beating until blended. Stir in pecans.

Drop dough by level tablespoonfuls 2 inches apart onto lightly greased baking sheets.

Bake at 350° for 12 to 15 minutes. Cool cookies slightly on baking sheets; remove to wire racks to cool completely. Yield: 3 dozen.

COFFEE BEAN COOKIES

These rich drop cookies are studded with chocolate-covered coffee beans, chunks of toffee candy bars, and almonds.

- ½ cup butter, softened
- ½ cup shortening
- ¾ cup sugar
- ¾ cup firmly packed brown sugar
- 2 large eggs
- 1 teaspoon vanilla extract
- 2¼ cups all-purpose flour
- 1 teaspoon baking soda
- 1 teaspoon salt
- ½ teaspoon ground cinnamon
- 1 cup chopped almonds, toasted
- 3 (2-ounce) packages chocolate-covered coffee beans (1 cup)
- 4 (1.4-ounce) English toffee candy bars, chopped (about 1 cup)

Beat butter and shortening at medium speed with an electric mixer until creamy; gradually add sugars, beating well. Add eggs and vanilla; beat well.

Combine flour and next 3 ingredients; add to butter mixture, beating well.

Stir in chopped almonds, chocolate-covered coffee beans, and chopped English toffee candy bars. Cover and chill dough, if desired.

Drop dough by heaping teaspoonfuls onto ungreased baking sheets.

Bake at 350° for 10 to 11 minutes or until golden. Cool 1 minute on baking sheets; remove to wire racks to cool completely. Yield: 4 dozen.

Coffee Bean Cookies

SPICED APPLE-OATMEAL COOKIES

- 1/4 cup butter or margarine, softened
- 1/2 cup shortening
- 1 1/4 cups firmly packed dark brown sugar
- 3/4 cup sugar
- 2 large eggs
- 1 1/4 cups cinnamon applesauce
- 1 1/2 teaspoons vanilla extract
- 1 1/2 cups all-purpose flour
- 1 teaspoon baking soda
- 1/2 teaspoon salt
- 2 teaspoons ground cinnamon
- 1/2 teaspoon ground nutmeg
- 1/4 teaspoon ground cloves
- 3 cups uncooked quick-cooking oats
- 1 cup chopped dried apple
- 1 cup raisins

Beat butter and shortening at medium speed with an electric mixer until creamy; add sugars, beating well. Add eggs, applesauce, and vanilla, beating well.

Combine flour, baking soda, salt, and spices; gradually add to butter mixture, beating well.

Stir in oats, chopped dried apple, and raisins.

Drop dough by tablespoonfuls 2 inches apart onto ungreased baking sheets.

Bake at 350° for 12 minutes. Cool 1 minute on baking sheets; remove to wire racks to cool completely. Yield: 4 dozen.

CHUNKY CHOCOLATE-TOFFEE COOKIES

When you need crowd-pleasing cookies, bake a double batch of these.

- 1 cup hazelnuts or pecans
- 1 cup unsalted butter, softened
- ¾ cup firmly packed brown sugar
- ½ cup sugar
- 2 large eggs
- 1 tablespoon vanilla extract
- 2¾ cups all-purpose flour
- 1½ teaspoons baking powder
- ½ teaspoon baking soda
- ½ teaspoon salt
- 4 (1.4-ounce) English toffee candy bars, chopped (about 1 cup)
- 2 (11.5-ounce) packages semisweet chocolate chunks

Toast hazelnuts in a shallow pan at 350°, stirring occasionally, 5 to 10 minutes or until skins split. Rub nuts in a cloth towel to remove skins.

Beat butter at medium speed with an electric mixer until creamy; gradually add sugars, beating well. Add eggs and vanilla, beating well.

Combine flour and next 3 ingredients; add to butter mixture, beating at low speed until blended. Stir in candy bars, chocolate chunks, and nuts.

Drop dough by heaping tablespoonfuls 1½ inches apart onto ungreased baking sheets.

Bake at 350° for 10 minutes or until cookies are lightly browned. Cool cookies slightly on baking sheets; remove to wire racks to cool completely. Yield: 4 dozen.

Sugar Crinkles
(page 64)

chapter

3

shaped

cookies

SUGAR CRINKLES

Your kitchen will smell like a bakery when you make these tender treasures (shown on page 62).

1 cup shortening
1½ cups sugar
2 large eggs
1 teaspoon lemon extract
1 teaspoon vanilla extract
2½ cups all-purpose flour
2 teaspoons baking powder
½ teaspoon salt
¼ cup sugar

Beat shortening and 1½ cups sugar at medium speed with an electric mixer until fluffy. Add eggs and flavorings, beating until blended.

Combine flour, baking powder, and salt; gradually add to shortening mixture, beating well. Cover and chill dough.

Shape dough into 1-inch balls; roll in ¼ cup sugar. Place on ungreased baking sheets.

Bake at 350° for 8 to 9 minutes or until barely golden. Cool 2 minutes on baking sheets; remove to wire racks to cool completely. Yield: about 5½ dozen.

PECAN-BUTTER COOKIES

A hint of lemon comes through in these simple butter cookies. They're good plain, and just plain good.

- 1 cup butter or margarine, softened
- 1 cup sugar
- 2 egg yolks
- ¾ teaspoon vanilla extract
- ¾ teaspoon almond extract
- ½ teaspoon lemon extract
- 2 cups all-purpose flour
- 1 teaspoon baking powder
- ¼ teaspoon salt
- ¾ cup pecan halves

Beat butter at medium speed with an electric mixer until creamy; gradually add sugar, beating well. Add egg yolks, 1 at a time, beating well after each addition. Stir in flavorings.

Combine flour, baking powder, and salt. Add to butter mixture, beating well.

Shape dough into 1-inch balls; place about 2 inches apart on ungreased baking sheets. Press a pecan half into center of each cookie.

Bake at 300° for 17 minutes or until edges are barely golden. Remove to wire racks to cool completely. Yield: 4 dozen.

HAZELNUT CRINKLE COOKIES

½ cup chopped hazelnuts
1 (13-ounce) jar chocolate-hazelnut spread
¼ cup shortening
1⅓ cups sugar
2 large eggs
1 teaspoon vanilla extract
3 cups all-purpose flour
2 teaspoons baking powder
½ teaspoon salt
⅓ cup milk
2 cups finely chopped hazelnuts
Sifted powdered sugar

Toast ½ cup chopped hazelnuts in a shallow pan at 350° for 5 to 10 minutes or until nuts smell fragrant. Set aside.

Beat chocolate-hazelnut spread and shortening at medium speed with an electric mixer until blended. Gradually add 1⅓ cups sugar, beating well. Add eggs and vanilla; beat until blended.

Combine flour, baking powder, and salt; add to chocolate-hazelnut mixture alternately with milk, beginning and ending with flour mixture. Stir in ½ cup toasted hazelnuts.

Shape dough into 1-inch balls; roll balls in finely chopped hazelnuts, and then in powdered sugar. Place 2 inches apart on lightly greased baking sheets.

Bake at 375° for 8 to 10 minutes or until set. Remove to wire racks to cool completely. Yield: 6 dozen.

RASPBERRY SWIRL COOKIES

- ½ cup butter or margarine, softened
- 1 cup sugar
- 1 large egg
- 1 teaspoon vanilla extract
- 2¼ cups all-purpose flour
- 1 teaspoon baking powder
- ¼ teaspoon salt
- ½ cup flaked coconut
- ½ cup raspberry jam
- ¼ cup finely chopped walnuts

Beat butter at medium speed with an electric mixer until creamy; gradually add sugar, beating well. Add egg and vanilla; beat well.

Combine flour, baking powder, and salt; gradually add to butter mixture, beating well. Shape dough into a ball; cover and chill at least 2 hours.

Roll dough into a 12- x 9-inch rectangle on floured wax paper. Combine coconut, jam, and walnuts; spread evenly over dough to within ½ inch of edges. Roll up dough, starting at long side and peeling wax paper from dough while rolling. Pinch side seam to seal. (Leave ends open.) Wrap roll in wax paper, and freeze until firm.

Unwrap dough, and cut into ¼-inch-thick slices; place slices 2 inches apart on parchment paper-lined baking sheets.

Bake at 375° for 10 to 12 minutes or until edges are lightly browned. Cool 1 minute on baking sheets; remove to wire racks to cool completely. Yield: 4 dozen.

Peppermint Crescents

PEPPERMINT CRESCENTS

These peppermint-topped buttery crescents will melt in your mouth.

1 cup butter, softened
⅔ cup sifted powdered sugar
1 teaspoon peppermint extract
⅛ teaspoon salt
2½ cups all-purpose flour
2 cups sifted powdered sugar, divided
2½ tablespoons milk
¼ teaspoon peppermint extract
Coarsely crushed hard peppermint candy

Beat butter at medium speed with an electric mixer until creamy. Add ⅔ cup powdered sugar, 1 teaspoon peppermint extract, and salt; beat well. Gradually add flour to butter mixture, beating at low speed just until blended after each addition. Divide dough into thirds; cover and chill 30 minutes.

Working with 1 portion of dough at a time, divide each portion into 12 pieces. Roll each piece into a 2-inch log; curve ends of each log to form a crescent. Place crescents 2 inches apart on lightly greased baking sheets.

Bake at 325° for 18 minutes or until lightly browned. Cool 1 minute on baking sheets. Carefully roll warm cookies in 1 cup powdered sugar, and then cool completely on wire racks.

Combine remaining 1 cup powdered sugar, milk, and ¼ teaspoon peppermint extract, stirring until smooth. Drizzle icing over cookies; sprinkle with crushed peppermint, pressing gently. Let icing set before serving. Store cookies in an airtight container. Yield: 3 dozen.

RED CURRANT THUMBPRINTS

Red currant jelly dollops Christmas color onto these pecan-coated thumbprint cookies.

1 cup butter, softened
¾ cup sugar
2 large eggs, separated
1 teaspoon almond extract
2 cups all-purpose flour
¼ teaspoon salt
1¼ teaspoons ground cinnamon
1¼ cups finely chopped pecans
Red currant jelly

Beat butter at medium speed with an electric mixer until creamy. Gradually add sugar, beating well. Add egg yolks and almond extract, beating until blended.

Combine flour, salt, and cinnamon. Add flour mixture to butter mixture, blending at low speed. Cover and chill dough 1 hour.

Shape dough into 1-inch balls. Lightly beat egg whites. Dip each ball in egg white; roll in pecans. Place 2 inches apart on ungreased baking sheets. Press thumb in each cookie to make an indentation.

Bake at 350° for 15 minutes. Cool 1 minute on baking sheets; remove to wire racks to cool completely. Press centers again with thumb while cookies are still warm; fill center of each cookie with jelly. Yield: about 3½ dozen.

CARAMEL-FILLED CHOCOLATE COOKIES

This chocolaty cookie, complete with a surprise caramel filling, definitely falls into the best-ever category.

- 1 cup butter or margarine, softened
- 1 cup sugar
- 1 cup firmly packed brown sugar
- 2 large eggs
- 2 teaspoons vanilla extract
- 2¼ cups all-purpose flour
- 1 teaspoon baking soda
- ¾ cup cocoa
- 1 cup finely chopped pecans, divided
- 1 tablespoon sugar
- 1 (9-ounce) package chewy caramels in milk chocolate

Beat butter at medium speed with an electric mixer until creamy; gradually add sugars, beating well. Add eggs and vanilla; beat well.

Combine flour, baking soda, and cocoa; gradually add to butter mixture, beating well. Stir in ½ cup pecans. Cover and chill dough at least 2 hours. Combine remaining ½ cup pecans and 1 tablespoon sugar.

Divide dough into 4 equal portions. Work with 1 portion at a time, storing remaining dough in refrigerator.

Divide each portion into 12 pieces. Quickly press each piece of dough around a caramel; roll into a ball. Dip 1 side of ball in pecan mixture. Place balls, pecan side up, 2 inches apart on ungreased baking sheets.

Bake at 375° for 8 minutes. (Cookies will look soft.) Cool 1 minute on baking sheets; remove to wire racks to cool completely. Yield: 4 dozen.

CINNAMON-PECAN ICEBOX COOKIES

1 cup butter or margarine, softened
¾ cup sugar
¼ cup firmly packed brown sugar
1 large egg
1 teaspoon vanilla extract
2¼ cups all-purpose flour
1½ teaspoons baking powder
½ teaspoon salt
1 cup finely chopped pecans
¼ cup sugar
1½ teaspoons ground cinnamon

Beat butter at medium speed with an electric mixer until creamy; gradually add ¾ cup sugar and brown sugar, beating well. Add egg and vanilla, beating well.

Combine flour, baking powder, and salt; add to butter mixture, beating well at medium speed. Stir in pecans. Cover and chill dough 2 hours.

Shape dough into 2 (6-inch) logs. Wrap logs in wax paper, and freeze until firm.

Combine ¼ cup sugar and cinnamon on a shallow plate; stir well. Unwrap frozen dough, and roll in sugar mixture.

Slice frozen dough into ¼-inch-thick slices; place slices on ungreased baking sheets.

Bake at 350° for 12 to 14 minutes or until lightly browned. Remove cookies to wire racks to cool completely. Yield: 4 dozen.

Cinnamon-Pecan
Icebox Cookies

PECAN BISCOTTI

1¾ cups all-purpose flour
1¼ teaspoons baking powder
¼ teaspoon salt
½ cup yellow cornmeal
1 cup finely chopped pecans
2 large eggs, lightly beaten
¾ cup sugar
½ cup vegetable oil
Dash of almond extract or vanilla extract

Combine first 5 ingredients in a large bowl. Combine eggs and remaining 3 ingredients; gradually add to flour mixture, stirring just until dry ingredients are moistened.

Place dough on a lightly floured surface; divide in half. With lightly floured hands, shape each half into a 12-inch log. Place logs 3 inches apart on a lightly greased baking sheet. Bake at 350° for 25 minutes; cool 10 minutes on baking sheet.

Cut each log crosswise into ¾-inch-thick slices, using a serrated knife. Place slices, cut side down, on ungreased baking sheets.

Bake at 350° for 12 minutes, turning cookies once. Remove to wire racks to cool completely. Yield: 2 dozen.

PEANUT BUTTER FINGERS

Crunchy peanut butter and wheat germ give texture and nutty flavor to these little cookie logs.

1 cup extra-crunchy peanut butter
¾ cup firmly packed brown sugar
½ cup butter, softened
¼ cup honey
½ teaspoon vanilla extract
1 large egg
1½ cups all-purpose flour
½ teaspoon baking soda
½ teaspoon salt
½ cup wheat germ
1½ cups (9 ounces) semisweet chocolate morsels, melted

Beat first 6 ingredients at medium speed with an electric mixer until creamy. Combine flour and next 3 ingredients. Gradually add to butter mixture, beating well.

Shape dough into 1-inch balls. Roll balls into 2½-inch logs. Place logs 2 inches apart on ungreased baking sheets.

Bake at 325° for 12 minutes or until lightly browned. Cool 1 minute on baking sheets; remove to wire racks to cool completely. When logs are cool, dip 1 end of each cookie into melted chocolate morsels. Return cookies to wire racks, and let stand until chocolate is firm. Yield: 4 dozen.

Orange-Date-
Nut Cookies

ORANGE-DATE-NUT COOKIES

Here's a great gift cookie to mail—or to keep and enjoy with a cup of hot tea.

1 (10-ounce) package chopped dates
1 teaspoon grated orange rind
1 tablespoon orange juice
1 cup butter or margarine, softened
1½ cups sugar
1 large egg
1 teaspoon vanilla extract
2½ cups all-purpose flour
1½ teaspoons baking powder
½ teaspoon salt
1 cup finely chopped toasted pecans, divided

Line a 9- x 5-inch loafpan with aluminum foil, allowing foil to extend over edges of pan.

Position knife blade in food processor bowl; add first 3 ingredients. Process 45 seconds or until dates are finely chopped.

Beat butter at medium speed with a heavy-duty electric mixer until blended. Gradually add sugar, beating until blended. Add egg and vanilla; beat well.

Combine flour, baking powder, and salt; gradually add to butter mixture, beating at low speed just until blended.

Divide dough into 3 portions. Knead ½ cup pecans into 1 portion of dough; press dough into prepared pan. Knead date mixture into 1 portion of dough; press in pan over pecan dough. Knead remaining ½ cup pecans into remaining portion of dough; press in pan over date dough. Cover and chill at least 2 hours.

Invert loafpan onto a cutting board; remove and discard aluminum foil. Cut dough lengthwise into 4 sections. Cut each section of dough crosswise into ¼-inch slices. Place slices 1½ inches apart on lightly greased baking sheets.

Bake at 350° for 9 to 10 minutes or until lightly browned. Cool slightly on baking sheets; remove to wire racks to cool completely. Yield: 8 dozen.

ALMOND FORTUNE COOKIES

- ½ cup all-purpose flour
- ¼ cup sugar
- 1 tablespoon cornstarch
- Dash of salt
- ¼ cup vegetable oil
- ¾ teaspoon vanilla extract
- ½ teaspoon lemon extract
- 2 egg whites
- 2 tablespoons ground blanched almonds
- 18 paper fortunes (2½- x ½-inch)

Combine first 4 ingredients in a medium mixing bowl; stir well. Add oil and next 3 ingredients, beating well at medium speed with an electric mixer until smooth. Stir in almonds.

Spoon 1 heaping teaspoonful batter onto a well-greased baking sheet; spread batter to a 3- to 3½-inch circle with back of a spoon.

Bake cookies, 2 at a time, at 325° for 8 to 9 minutes or until golden. (Let baking sheet cool completely between batches, and regrease baking sheet each time.)

Working quickly, remove 1 cookie at a time with a wide spatula. Place a paper fortune in center of each cookie; fold cookie in half. Using the handle of a spoon, indent each cookie in the middle of the fold, pulling the ends of the cookie towards the center. Place each cookie in an ungreased muffin cup to hold its shape while cooling. (If cookie cools before it is shaped, reheat in oven about 1 minute.) Cool completely. Store cookies in an airtight container. Yield: 1½ dozen.

Almond Fortune Cookies

LEMON THYME COOKIES

If you have a green thumb for growing herbs, try these cookies in the summer when lemon thyme is thriving and fragrant in the garden.

1 cup butter or margarine, softened
1½ cups sugar
2 large eggs
2½ cups all-purpose flour
2 teaspoons cream of tartar
½ teaspoon salt
½ cup chopped fresh lemon thyme

Beat butter at medium speed with an electric mixer until creamy; gradually add sugar, beating well. Add eggs, 1 at a time, beating until blended after each addition.

Combine flour, cream of tartar, and salt; gradually add to butter mixture. Beat at low speed until blended after each addition. Stir in lemon thyme.

Shape dough into 2 (10-inch) logs; wrap each log in wax paper, and chill at least 2 hours.

Unwrap dough; cut each log into ½-inch-thick slices, and place on lightly greased baking sheets.

Bake at 350° for 10 minutes. Remove to wire racks to cool. Yield: 3½ dozen.

MOLASSES-SUGAR COOKIES

- ¾ cup shortening
- 1 cup sugar
- ¼ cup molasses
- 1 large egg
- 2¼ cups all-purpose flour
- 2 teaspoons baking soda
- ½ teaspoon salt
- 1 teaspoon ground ginger
- 1 teaspoon ground cinnamon
- ½ teaspoon ground cloves
- ¼ cup sugar

Melt shortening in a large saucepan over low heat. Remove from heat; cool. Stir in 1 cup sugar, molasses, and egg.

Combine flour and next 5 ingredients in a large mixing bowl; gradually add sugar mixture, beating at medium speed with an electric mixer until blended. Shape dough into 1-inch balls; roll in ¼ cup sugar. Place 2 inches apart on lightly greased baking sheets.

Bake at 375° for 8 to 10 minutes. Remove to wire racks to cool. Yield: about 4 dozen.

Chocolate-Orange
Cream Fingers (page 84)

chapter

4

bar

cookies

CHOCOLATE-ORANGE CREAM FINGERS

We spiked these brownies (shown on page 82) with Grand Marnier; orange extract also works well.

- 4 large eggs
- 2 cups sugar
- 1 cup all-purpose flour
- 1 cup cocoa
- 1 cup butter or margarine, melted
- 1½ teaspoons Grand Marnier or ½ teaspoon orange extract
- 3 (1-ounce) squares unsweetened chocolate
- 3 tablespoons butter or margarine
- Orange Cream Frosting

Beat eggs with a wire whisk until thick and frothy. Add sugar; stir well. Combine flour and cocoa; gradually stir into egg mixture. Stir in 1 cup melted butter and liqueur. Pour into a greased 15- x 10-inch jellyroll pan.

Bake at 350° for 20 to 22 minutes or until a wooden pick inserted in center comes out clean. Cool in pan on a wire rack.

Heat chocolate squares and 3 tablespoons butter in a saucepan over low heat, stirring constantly, until melted. Cool.

Spread frosting over uncut brownies. Drizzle cooled chocolate over frosting. Dip a small spatula in hot water; wipe dry. Using warm spatula, spread chocolate thinly to cover frosting completely. Let stand until chocolate is set. Cut into thin bars. Store in refrigerator. Yield: 4 dozen.

ORANGE CREAM FROSTING

- ¼ cup butter or margarine, softened
- 2¾ cups sifted powdered sugar
- 1 teaspoon grated orange rind
- 1½ tablespoons orange juice
- 1 tablespoon Grand Marnier or orange juice

Beat butter at medium speed with an electric mixer until creamy; gradually add sugar, beating well. Add orange rind, juice, and liqueur; beat until blended. Yield: 1¼ cups.

NO-BAKE GRANOLA BARS

These granola bars resemble the ever-popular marshmallow squares, but the peanut butter and chocolate morsels make them unforgettable.

2½ cups crisp rice cereal
2 cups uncooked quick-cooking oats
½ cup raisins
½ cup firmly packed brown sugar
½ cup light corn syrup
½ cup peanut butter
1 teaspoon vanilla extract
½ cup milk chocolate morsels

Combine first 3 ingredients in a large bowl; set aside.

Bring brown sugar and syrup to a boil in a small saucepan over medium-high heat, stirring constantly; remove from heat. Stir in peanut butter and vanilla until blended.

Pour peanut butter mixture over cereal and raisins, stirring until coated; let stand 10 minutes. Stir in chocolate morsels.

Press into a lightly greased 13- x 9-inch pan (do not bake); cool completely in pan on a wire rack. Cut into bars. Yield: 4½ dozen.

WHITE CHOCOLATE-ALMOND BLONDIES

These chewy blonde brownies are full of almonds and buttery white chocolate bits.

2 cups all-purpose flour
1½ teaspoons baking powder
½ teaspoon salt
⅔ cup butter or margarine
1½ teaspoons instant coffee granules
2 cups firmly packed brown sugar
2 large eggs, lightly beaten
1 cup whole natural almonds, coarsely chopped and toasted
1 cup (6 ounces) white chocolate morsels or 6 ounces white chocolate, chopped

Combine first 3 ingredients in a medium bowl; set aside.

Melt butter in a large saucepan over medium-low heat. Add coffee granules, stirring until dissolved. Remove from heat. Add brown sugar and eggs; stir well. Gradually stir in flour mixture. Add almonds and white chocolate, stirring well. Spread batter in a lightly greased 13- x 9-inch pan.

Bake at 350° for 30 minutes. Cool completely in pan on a wire rack. Cut into squares. Yield: 2½ dozen.

White Chocolate-
Almond Blondies

Chocolate
Candy-Oat Bars

CHOCOLATE CANDY-OAT BARS

If M&M's are your thing, you'll love them in these fudgy bar cookies.

- 2 cups uncooked quick-cooking oats
- 1½ cups all-purpose flour
- 1 cup firmly packed brown sugar
- 1 cup chopped pecans
- 1 teaspoon baking soda
- ¼ teaspoon salt
- 1 cup butter or margarine, melted
- 1½ cups candy-coated chocolate pieces, divided
- 1 (14-ounce) can sweetened condensed milk

Combine first 6 ingredients, stirring well. Add butter, and stir or beat at low speed with an electric mixer until mixture is crumbly. Reserve 1½ cups crumb mixture; press remaining crumb mixture into a lightly greased 15- x 10-inch jellyroll pan. (Mixture will be thin in pan.)

Bake at 375° for 10 minutes. Cool on a wire rack. Reduce oven temperature to 350°.

Place 1 cup chocolate pieces in a microwave-safe bowl; microwave at HIGH 1 to 1½ minutes, stirring after 30 seconds.

Press chocolate pieces with back of a spoon to mash them. (The candies will almost be melted with pieces of color coating still visible.) Stir in condensed milk. Spread mixture evenly over crust in pan, leaving a ½-inch border on all sides.

Combine reserved 1½ cups crumb mixture and remaining ½ cup chocolate pieces. Sprinkle over chocolate mixture; press lightly.

Bake at 350° for 18 to 20 minutes or until golden; cool completely in pan on a wire rack. Cut into bars. Yield: 4 dozen.

KEY LIME BARS WITH MACADAMIA CRUST

2 cups all-purpose flour
½ cup firmly packed brown sugar
⅔ cup chopped macadamia nuts
7 tablespoons butter, cubed
½ teaspoon salt
¾ cup sugar
½ cup Key lime juice
1 envelope unflavored gelatin
2 tablespoons Key lime juice
1 (14-ounce) can sweetened condensed milk
1 teaspoon grated lime rind
Green and yellow liquid food coloring (optional)
2½ cups whipping cream, whipped
Garnishes: grated lime rind and Key lime rind, fresh raspberries

Process first 5 ingredients in a food processor until thoroughly blended and nuts are ground. Press into a greased heavy-duty aluminum foil-lined 13- x 9-inch pan, letting edges of foil extend beyond edges of pan.

Bake at 350° for 18 minutes or until barely golden. Cool in pan on a wire rack.

Heat ¾ cup sugar and ½ cup lime juice over low heat, stirring until sugar dissolves. Remove from heat; set aside.

Sprinkle gelatin over 2 tablespoons lime juice in a medium bowl. Stir gelatin mixture, and let stand 3 to 5 minutes.

Add hot mixture, stirring until gelatin dissolves. Whisk in sweetened condensed milk and 1 teaspoon grated lime rind. Add 1 drop green and 3 drops yellow food coloring, if desired.

Place bowl in a larger bowl filled with ice; gently whisk mixture 10 minutes or until partially set.

Fold lime mixture into whipped cream. Pour evenly over baked crust; cover and chill 8 hours. Carefully lift foil out of pan. Cut dessert into diamond shapes or bars. Garnish, if desired. Yield: 2 dozen.

Key Lime Bars with
Macadamia Crust

LEMON HEARTS

2 cups all-purpose flour
½ cup sifted powdered sugar
1 cup butter or margarine, softened
1 teaspoon vanilla extract
2 cups sugar
2 tablespoons cornstarch
5 large eggs, lightly beaten
1 tablespoon grated lemon rind
¼ cup plus 2 tablespoons lemon juice
2 tablespoons butter or margarine, melted
2 to 4 tablespoons powdered sugar
Garnishes: lemon rind knots, fresh raspberries

Combine first 4 ingredients; beat at medium speed with an electric mixer until blended. Pat mixture into a greased 13- x 9-inch baking dish. Bake at 350° for 18 minutes or until golden.

Combine 2 cups sugar and cornstarch. Add eggs and next 3 ingredients; beat well. Pour mixture over crust.

Bake at 350° for 20 to 25 minutes or until set. Cool completely. Chill well.

Sift 2 to 4 tablespoons powdered sugar over top. Cut into hearts or flowers, using a cookie cutter; or cut into bars. Garnish, if desired. Yield: 14 hearts, 14 flowers, or 2½ dozen bars.

Lemon Hearts

CREAM CHEESE SWIRL BROWNIES

1 (4-ounce) package sweet baking chocolate
3 tablespoons butter or margarine
½ (8-ounce) package cream cheese, softened
2 tablespoons butter or margarine, softened
¼ cup sifted powdered sugar
3 large eggs
1 tablespoon all-purpose flour
½ teaspoon vanilla extract
¾ cup sugar
½ cup all-purpose flour
½ teaspoon baking powder
¼ teaspoon salt
1½ teaspoons vanilla extract

Melt chocolate and 3 tablespoons butter in a saucepan over low heat, stirring constantly. Remove from heat; set aside.

Beat cream cheese and 2 tablespoons butter at medium speed with an electric mixer until creamy; gradually add powdered sugar, beating well. Add 1 egg, 1 tablespoon flour, and ½ teaspoon vanilla, beating well. Set cream cheese batter aside.

Beat remaining 2 eggs at medium speed until thick and pale; gradually add ¾ cup sugar, beating until thickened.

Combine ½ cup flour, baking powder, and salt; gradually add to egg mixture, beating well. Stir in chocolate mixture and 1½ teaspoons vanilla.

Spread 1 cup chocolate batter in a greased 8-inch square pan. Spoon cream cheese batter over chocolate batter in pan; top with remaining chocolate batter. Swirl with a knife to create a marbled effect.

Bake at 350° for 35 minutes or until done. Cool completely in pan on a wire rack, and cut into squares. Yield: 16 brownies.

MINT CHOCOLATE CRUMBLE BARS

- 1 (10-ounce) package teddy bear-shaped chocolate graham cracker cookies, crushed (about 2½ cups)
- ½ cup butter or margarine, melted
- 3 (1.55-ounce) minty milk chocolate bars with crunchy cookie bits, chopped
- 6 (1-ounce) squares white baking bar or white chocolate, chopped
- 1 cup chopped pistachios or pecans
- 1 cup flaked coconut
- 1 cup (6 ounces) semisweet chocolate morsels
- 1 large egg, lightly beaten
- 1 (14-ounce) can sweetened condensed milk

Combine cookie crumbs and melted butter; stir well. Press crumb mixture into a lightly greased 13- x 9-inch pan. Bake at 350° for 15 minutes.

Sprinkle chopped candy bars and next 4 ingredients over baked crust.

Combine egg and sweetened condensed milk; pour mixture over chocolate morsels in crust.

Bake at 350° for 35 minutes. Cool completely in pan on a wire rack, and cut into bars. Yield: 2½ dozen.

Gooey Turtle Bars
(page 98)

chapter 5

simple cookies

Short ingredient lists and convenience products distinguish the ultraeasy cookies in this chapter.

GOOEY TURTLE BARS

You're just five ingredients away from tasting these decadent chocolate-caramel bars (shown on page 96).

2 cups graham cracker crumbs or vanilla wafer crumbs
½ cup butter or margarine, melted
2 cups (12 ounces) semisweet chocolate morsels
1 cup pecan pieces
1 (12-ounce) jar caramel topping

Combine graham cracker crumbs and butter in an ungreased 13- x 9-inch pan; stir and press firmly into bottom of pan. Sprinkle with chocolate morsels and pecans.

Remove lid from caramel topping; microwave at HIGH 1 to 1½ minutes or until hot, stirring after 30 seconds. Drizzle over pecans.

Bake at 350° for 15 minutes or until chocolate morsels melt; cool in pan on a wire rack. Chill at least 30 minutes; cut into bars. Yield: 2 dozen.

CAKE MIX COOKIES

- 1 (18.25-ounce) package devil's food cake mix
- 1 large egg, lightly beaten
- ½ (8-ounce) container frozen whipped topping, thawed
- 1 cup chopped pecans (optional)
- ½ cup sifted powdered sugar

Combine first 3 ingredients, stirring well (dough will be sticky). Stir in pecans, if desired.

Dust hands with powdered sugar, and shape dough into ¾-inch balls. Coat balls with powdered sugar, and place 2 inches apart on ungreased baking sheets.

Bake at 350° for 10 to 12 minutes or until done; remove to wire racks to cool. Yield: about 5 dozen.

QUICK CHOCOLATE COOKIES

You won't find a cookie recipe much easier to make ahead than this one. You can freeze the balls of dough up to six months. Just thaw and bake . . . and enjoy!

- ¾ cup biscuit mix
- 1 (3.9-ounce) package chocolate fudge instant pudding mix
- ¼ cup vegetable oil
- 1 large egg

Combine all ingredients in a mixing bowl; beat at medium speed with an electric mixer until blended.

Shape dough into 1-inch balls. Place on baking sheets, and freeze, if desired. Place frozen dough balls in an airtight container, and freeze up to 6 months. Thaw in refrigerator before baking. Place 2 inches apart on lightly greased baking sheets.

Bake at 350° for 8 minutes. Cool 1 minute on baking sheets; remove to wire racks to cool completely. Yield: 2 dozen.

GINGERBREAD FRUITCAKE COOKIES

This little drop cookie packs a big punch of ginger flavor.

- 1 (14-ounce) package gingerbread mix*
- ¼ cup plus 2 tablespoons water
- ¼ cup butter or margarine, melted
- 1 (4-ounce) container candied orange peel
- ½ cup golden raisins
- ½ cup chopped pecans
- 1½ cups sifted powdered sugar
- 2½ tablespoons lemon juice or orange juice

Combine first 3 ingredients, stirring until smooth. Fold in candied orange peel, raisins, and pecans.

Drop dough by rounded teaspoonfuls onto lightly greased baking sheets.

Bake at 350° for 10 minutes. Cool slightly on baking sheets; remove to wire racks to cool completely.

Combine powdered sugar and lemon juice, stirring until smooth. Drizzle over cooled cookies. Yield: 4 dozen.

*For gingerbread mix, we used Dromedary.

Praline Grahams

PRALINE GRAHAMS

This is a delicious cross between a bar cookie and candy. It's an easy and excellent dress-up for any flavor graham cracker—regular, chocolate, or cinnamon. Use margarine instead of butter for best results with the syrupy coating.

12 whole regular graham crackers or chocolate graham crackers*
¾ cup margarine
½ cup sugar
1 cup chopped pecans

Break graham crackers in half into squares. Arrange graham cracker squares with edges touching in an ungreased 15- x 10-inch jelly-roll pan.

Melt margarine in a saucepan over medium heat; stir in sugar and chopped pecans. Bring to a boil, stirring constantly. Cook 5 minutes, stirring often. Remove from heat. Working quickly, spread syrupy mixture evenly over graham crackers in pan.

Bake at 300° for 12 minutes. Remove from pan to cool completely on a wire rack. Yield: 2 dozen.

* For graham crackers, we used Nabisco HoneyMaid. The number of graham crackers per package varies from 10 to 12 depending on the brand. No matter which brand you buy, you'll need at least 1 package from a box for this recipe.

CHOCOLATE MACAROONS

Coconut and almond are flavors common to chewy macaroon cookies. No electric mixer's required in this chocolate version—just stir with a spoon.

- 1 cup sweetened condensed milk
- ½ cup all-purpose flour
- ½ teaspoon almond extract or vanilla extract
- 1 (7-ounce) can flaked coconut
- 1 (3.9-ounce) package chocolate instant pudding mix

Combine all ingredients, stirring well.

Drop dough by rounded teaspoonfuls onto lightly greased baking sheets.

Bake at 325° for 10 to 12 minutes. Cool 1 minute on baking sheets; remove to wire racks to cool completely. Yield: 3½ dozen.

TRIPLE-TREAT BARS

Once you melt the morsels, there's no more cooking needed for these butterscotch bars.

Vegetable cooking spray
2 cups (12 ounces) butterscotch morsels
½ cup plus 2 tablespoons creamy peanut butter
4 cups granola
1½ cups candy-coated chocolate pieces

Coat a 13- x 9-inch pan with cooking spray; line with wax paper.

Cook butterscotch morsels and peanut butter in a heavy saucepan over low heat until morsels melt.

Combine granola and chocolate pieces in a bowl; pour butterscotch mixture over granola and candy, stirring to coat.

Spread mixture in prepared pan. Cover and chill until firm. Cut into bars. Yield: 1½ dozen.

CHEWY ALMOND-FUDGE BARS

Coconut candy bars and toasted almonds give these fudgy brownies their personality. If you like firm bars, chill them.

- 1 (19.8-ounce) package chewy fudge brownie mix*
- 3 tablespoons vegetable oil
- 1 cup sweetened condensed milk
- 14 miniature dark chocolate coconut candy bars, chopped (1¼ cups)*
- ¾ cup chopped natural almonds, toasted

Prepare brownie mix according to package directions, reducing vegetable oil to 3 tablespoons; pour into a lightly greased 13- x 9-inch pan.

Pour sweetened condensed milk over batter; sprinkle with chopped candy bars and almonds.

Bake at 350° for 36 to 38 minutes. Cool completely in pan on a wire rack. Cut into bars. Yield: 2 dozen.

*For brownie mix, we used Duncan Hines. For miniature dark chocolate coconut candy bars, we used Mounds.

Chewy Almond-
Fudge Bars

COCONUT DESSERT BARS

These chewy bar cookies are best served warm.

- 2 (7.2-ounce) packages home-style fluffy white frosting mix
- ⅓ cup all-purpose flour
- ¼ teaspoon salt
- ½ cup milk
- 2 tablespoons butter or margarine, melted
- 1 teaspoon vanilla extract
- 3 large eggs
- 1⅓ cups flaked coconut

Combine first 7 ingredients; beat at medium speed with an electric mixer 2 minutes or until well blended. Stir in flaked coconut. Pour mixture into a greased and floured 13- x 9-inch pan.

Bake at 350° for 25 to 30 minutes; cover with aluminum foil, and bake 5 to 10 more minutes or until a wooden pick inserted in center comes out clean. Cut into bars. Serve warm. Yield: 12 to 15 bars.

EASY REINDEER COOKIES

1 (20-ounce) package refrigerated sliceable peanut butter cookie dough
60 (2-inch) pretzel twists
60 semisweet chocolate morsels
30 red candy-coated chocolate pieces

Freeze peanut butter cookie dough 15 minutes.

Cut dough into 30 (¼-inch-thick) slices. Place 4 inches apart on ungreased baking sheets. Using thumb and forefinger, pinch in each slice about two-thirds of the way down to shape face.

Press a pretzel on each side of larger end for antlers. Press in chocolate morsels for eyes.

Bake at 350° for 9 to 11 minutes or until lightly browned. Remove from oven; press in red candy for each nose. Cool 2 minutes on baking sheets; remove cookies to wire racks to cool completely. Yield: 2½ dozen.

INDEX

METRIC EQUIVALENTS

The recipes that appear in this cookbook use the standard United States method for measuring liquid and dry or solid ingredients (teaspoons, tablespoons, and cups). The information on this chart is provided to help cooks outside the U.S. successfully use these recipes. All equivalents are approximate.

EQUIVALENTS FOR DIFFERENT TYPES OF INGREDIENTS

A standard cup measure of a dry or solid ingredient will vary in weight depending on the type of ingredient. A standard cup of liquid is the same volume for any type of liquid. Use the following chart when converting standard cup measures to grams (weight) or milliliters (volume).

Standard Cup	Fine Powder (ex. flour)	Grain (ex. rice)	Granular (ex. sugar)	Liquid Solids (ex. butter)	Liquid (ex. milk)
1	140 g	150 g	190 g	200 g	240 ml
¾	105 g	113 g	143 g	150 g	180 ml
⅔	93 g	100 g	125 g	133 g	160 ml
½	70 g	75 g	95 g	100 g	120 ml
⅓	47 g	50 g	63 g	67 g	80 ml
¼	35 g	38 g	48 g	50 g	60 ml
⅛	18 g	19 g	24 g	25 g	30 ml

EQUIVALENTS FOR LIQUID INGREDIENTS BY VOLUME

¼ tsp							=	1 ml
½ tsp							=	2 ml
1 tsp							=	5 ml
3 tsp =	1 tbls				=	½ fl oz	=	15 ml
	2 tbls	=	⅛ cup		=	1 fl oz	=	30 ml
	4 tbls	=	¼ cup		=	2 fl oz	=	60 ml
	5⅓ tbls	=	⅓ cup		=	3 fl oz	=	80 ml
	8 tbls	=	½ cup		=	4 fl oz	=	120 ml
	10⅔ tbls	=	⅔ cup		=	5 fl oz	=	160 ml
	12 tbls	=	¾ cup		=	6 fl oz	=	180 ml
	16 tbls	=	1 cup		=	8 fl oz	=	240 ml
	1 pt	=	2 cups		=	16 fl oz	=	480 ml
	1 qt	=	4 cups		=	32 fl oz	=	960 ml
						33 fl oz	=	1000 ml = 1 liter

EQUIVALENTS FOR DRY INGREDIENTS BY WEIGHT

(To convert ounces to grams, multiply the number of ounces by 30.)

1 oz	=	1/16 lb	=	30 g
4 oz	=	¼ lb	=	120 g
8 oz	=	½ lb	=	240 g
12 oz	=	¾ lb	=	360 g
16 oz	=	1 lb	=	480 g

EQUIVALENTS FOR LENGTH

(To convert inches to centimeters, multiply the number of inches by 2.5.)

1 in		= 2.5 cm	
6 in	= ½ ft	= 15 cm	
12 in	= 1 ft	= 30 cm	
36 in	= 3 ft = 1 yd	= 90 cm	
40 in		= 100 cm	= 1 meter

EQUIVALENTS FOR COOKING/OVEN TEMPERATURES

	Fahrenheit	Celsius	Gas Mark
Freeze Water	32° F	0° C	
Room Temperature	68° F	20° C	
Boil Water	212° F	100° C	
Bake	325° F	160° C	3
	350° F	180° C	4
	375° F	190° C	5
	400° F	200° C	6
	425° F	220° C	7
	450° F	230° C	8
Broil			Grill